Richard Gwyn was born in Cardiff. He studied anthro Economics and became int languages and music of per years travelling on and arour. stays in Crete and Catalonia, forming enduring links with people, places and wooden boats. *Walking on Bones* is his fourth book of poetry. He has read his work at a variety of venues in Britain and the U.S.A., and has been involved in collaborations with visual artists in Wales, France and Spain.

PARTHIAN BOOKS

WALKING ON BONES

RICHARD GWYN

With drawings by Tessa Waite

PARTHIAN BOOKS

Parthian Books
53 Colum Road
Cardiff
CF10 3EF
www.parthianbooks.co.uk

First published in 2000.
All rights reserved.
Text © Richard Gwyn
Illustrations © Tessa Waite
ISBN 1 902638 06 9

Typeset in Sabon by NW.

Printed and bound by ColourBooks, Dublin 13,
Ireland.

The publishers would like to thank the Arts Council of
Wales for support in the publication of this book.

With support from the Parthian Collective.

Cover "Voyage" by Tessa Waite:
Ink and watercolour.

A CIP catalogue record for this book is available from
the British Library.

For Sioned and Rhiannon

Poetry Books by Richard Gwyn

Defying Gravity (1992)
One Night in Icarus Street (1995)
Stone Dog, Flower Red/Gos de Pedra, Flor Vermella (1995)

Poems from *Walking on Bones* have appeared in *Poetry Wales*, *Interchange* and *The Prose Poem: an international journal*.

CONTENTS

Once we have remembered, he said,

the moment of the thing remembered never passes.

The prickly pears not only have shape and taste – they enclose

a world of seeds and meaning within their hairy green fists,

they remember our procrastinations, they remember a 'later'

like a continuation of our own omissions . . . .

Yannis Ritsos *When the stranger comes*

Opening a Box

Who put these boxes here? An empty road. Scattered trees, none bearing fruit. A sky full of clouds that will not rain. No signs of human life. And yet these boxes, lined up precisely at the roadside, banked on the sandy soil in neat piles. Cardboard boxes with nothing written on them. No message or mark or company stamp. Plain brown card, with the tops folded over and tucked under. Whoever left them here knew it would not rain. I watch the boxes, as if expecting them to make the first move. I wait to see if anyone will come: if anyone is watching me watch the boxes, ready to leap out and confront me with an angry shout, come up close and face to face to swear at me, abuse me, curse me. I can hear the man, unshaven for a week, smell his sweat, watch the big vein throbbing in his neck. Silence. There is nothing here. Not even birds. So I listen for the sounds that are not here, and begin to hear them: distant shouting, a tractor, a crow's caw. The more I hear these absent sounds the deeper the silence grows. I approach the first box, loosen the flap. Open it.

Dusting

Dust is verbal. Billions of particles of god knows what, collecting on every surface, in every corner. Breeding bugs which, under the microscope, become grotesque and terrifying monsters. Dust that accumulates unnoticed and invisible until such time as it is noticed, and then suddenly you hear yourself observe that you had never realised quite how dusty this house was. Dust and cobwebs. Cobwebs undisturbed for months or even years. It all gets too much. You buy a feather duster, one with a telescopic handle. You open it out and wave it along the walls, under high shelves, into the most inaccessible reaches of the hall. Places where duster never dusted. Places where dust has piled thick. You run your finger down a ledge and it returns covered in the filth of 1976. Punk dust. It is now 2000. You wonder should you lick this dust, would you get a flavour of the past? What of medieval dust, Roman dust, good old Celtic sunset dust? Scoop it up and flog it off in coloured glass. Pagan dust, rhino dust, dinosaur dust. Millennium dust. Dust brushed by the saints. Christ dust. Buddha dust. The dust of our ancestors. Dust: if it weren't a metaphor for oblivion it could be a happy verb.

Sweeping

Try sweeping leaves. A long-handled, stiff-bristled modern brush or a witch's broom, take your pick. I favour the latter, simply because all through my childhood I wanted brooms that looked like that, but at home we always had the other sort. With the witch's broom, there's no room for complacency. I stand side-on to the sweeping gesture, elbows out, rather than pushing or pulling as the factory variety would have me do. Standing side-on to things is the witch's way. Everyone knows that malevolent witches sleep lying on their left side and approach their victims from the left. Good witches too, stand side-on to things, but from the right side, sometimes so sharply two-dimensional that they disappear altogether. I stand sweeping, pulling the broom from behind in long confident strokes, in the manner of a Cretan matriarch. Leaves, blood, half-eaten loaves of bread, snakeskins, spent cartridges, squirrels, pheasants, ponies, tractors. I remember once sweeping an entire city of leaves, its towers covered by the thick dank carpet of a thousand years' continuous fall. The piles of crinkled parchment, dislocated into whispers. Grabbing armfuls, tossing them skyward. Showering onto my head. The grit on my tongue. What moist secrets cram the worm and beetle-space? Sweeping in the October winds, leaves climb away like feathers, drifting and diving around my head. I sweep harder to catch up with myself. I bend to collect leaves

between my broom and a short plank. My little pile blows in all directions and I begin again.

Let's not discuss the colours of the leaves, but their smell. Let's not discuss the smell of leaves, but the mineral silence as they fall. There is nothing that defines autumn so absolutely as the smell of the colour of the sound of leaves being brushed as the evening sun falls behind black trees.

Lifting the Virgin

Her job is to keep the church clean, arrange the flowers, change the candles. At midday she cooks a meal for the priest. But her main concern is the well-being of the alabaster statues, especially the virgin. Last week, she tells me, they had to lift the statue of the virgin, move her awhile. 'You can't imagine how much she weighed', she smiles, as though discussing a defiant but beloved child. The wind has stopped. Everything is quiet. I walk with the priest to the village bar. Afterwards, in the square, the children gather round, playing and chatting, as though they have known me all their lives. I am a stranger, who has walked into this tiny place and soon will wander on. The woman in the church, the priest, the sky, the children, the little square with its tree and two swings. A conspiracy of nouns. But the effect is of a flow between one thing and the next, on a journey that has lost all points of reference and offers only the salvation of continuity. Lifting this lifesize model of the virgin provides a challenge to all that is unchanging in a village on a plain. She was so heavy. You can't imagine.

Guests

They came, the good travellers. Each of them a miracle of experience and observation. They had never read a travel book between them, far less written one. What these people did was slide unseen between the landscape and the setting sun. No surprise then that some of us considered them to be gods, who will occasionally disguise themselves as poor wayfarers in order to test us humans. You never know when they will call. A knock on the door one rainswept winter's night: a hunched silhouette stands shivering in the cold. Perilous, to scorn a god, or goddess. You let her in, offer her bread and cheese. In the morning she leaves, without a great display, but from that moment, miracles begin to happen in your life. Or take my case. High in the mountains, I lived alone. November. No thoroughfare, a bridle-track. The wind was howling around the cliffs. I put a log on the fire, filled my glass, and stretched out before the blaze. I had a sheepdog by the name of Filos. He started growling before I heard the knock. I went to the door. There were three of them, hooded. They were the good travellers.

Divers

One night in Christos' taverna two handsome boys invited my fiancée and me to the beach. We were to meet the next morning and would travel to the south of the island. The boys were polite, even formal, for Greeks of their age, treating my fiancée with unusual courtesy. They were in their early twenties and were connected to the military. They wore identical haircuts, and had an air of wellbeing, even of wealth. In the morning we arrived late, but the boys were waiting for us. They drove a white car. After travelling for over an hour the road came to an end. The boys carried gas cylinders and other gear down a steep dirt track to the sea. One of them slung a shotgun over his shoulder. At the beach they prepared for diving. I was handed the gun and a handful of cartridges; 'in case there's anything about'. Then they both went into the sea. My fiancée and I wandered along the beach. Sparse woodland offered no visible game. After a while we returned to the beach, found a shady spot and slept.

It was late afternoon when the boys returned from the sea. I don't know what happened to the hours. They spoke little, and showed us nothing. They continued to smile, but were never overbearing. They disappeared among the rocks and pools, busying about some obscure or secret task. Eventually, they collected their gear and motioned up the hill. It was time to go back to town.

One of the boys led the way, walking ten metres ahead, with the other accompanying us. Then, the boy who walked with us spoke. As soon as he had spoken, he turned into the other boy, the one who was walking ahead. I knew this, because at that instant, the boy who was ahead turned around to look at us, and he wore the face of the other one, the one who had been walking alongside us. Then it happened again; the one who walked beside us speaking, and immediately afterwards changing places with his friend. I do not remember what he said. We arrived at the car and unloaded the stuff. The boys were quieter now. They seemed tired by their swim, but they were still good-humoured.

We had not driven far when it happened a third time. My fiancée and I were in the back of the car. The one who was driving turned to speak to us, but no sooner had he finished his words than his face became his friend's face. This happened two or three more times. But the boys rarely spoke now. Back in town they took us to Christos' taverna and bought four Coca-Colas. They had stopped changing forms now that we were in a public place. They said they ate at Christos' place every night and would see us again soon. Then they left.

Later, I asked Christos about them. He said they had not been in his taverna before.

We never saw those boys again.

Camels Trotting

The soul travels at the speed of a trotting camel. Nowadays, when humans venture any distance, they choose a mode of transport significantly faster. The result? Lost souls, everywhere. Once when I flew from Athens to London, stayed ten days, and then returned, I reckoned that I passed my camel over Serbia, going in the opposite direction.

From the parched membranes of a feigned amnesia we conjure cowled faces against a starlit sky, folds of black silk, tufts of animal fur, dried blood, stale sweat, the cold night air of the desert crossing. The rhythm of this memory is that of a human heartbeat. The images retained by the eye are formed at exactly the right speed, and fade in time for the next one. Food is chewed and digested in the recommended way. Water only is drunk, and preciously conserved. The pernicious attributes of a godless world are simply unimagined. Animal images predominate. The deeper you dig, more beasties come at you. Everything has its animal corollary.

Tunis

One November night I took a seat outside a café whose tables were dotted across the square. Behind the café spread the medina, the city's nocturnal heart. I ordered tea, and was immediately joined by a couple of young men my own age, early twenties. They asked me who I was, and told me a little of themselves. We spoke French. I was enjoying the cool open space, the dappled light of the trees under streetlamps, the learning who each other was, though we would not meet again.

Three military trucks pulled up outside the café and soldiers cordoned off the terrace where we were sitting. Around fifty of us were rounded up into groups of four or five, and an officer moved between the soldiers, giving orders. When he came to our group my new friends told the officer I was a foreigner. The officer indicated that this information was of no interest to him, and that I was to be taken anyway. I surmised that, in his eyes, strangers were no less likely to be spies. One of the boys persisted in his protest, and a younger officer muttered something to his chief. They asked me for papers, which I gave them. The older officer inspected my passport reluctantly, then returned it. He told me that I needn't come with them. The soldiers bundled all the men into the backs of the three trucks. One of the young men from my table turned and shrugged in my direction as they led him off.

I sat alone outside the café for a while. The leaves rustled under the street lamps. I didn't finish my tea. Rising from the table, I went inside. The café-owner was chatting with a cop and another man. When I offered to pay, the café-owner took the money without looking at me.

Cleaning a Fish

In the modern home fish take on an alien aspect. You open the fridge door and there are eyes. This is not usual. Most food comes pre-packaged, in marked and colourful containers. Eyes are not part of the deal. Fresh fish are oblivious to this arrangement, go out of their way to upset the unsuspecting. This is why fishmongers (the word itself is disappearing) will ask you if you want your fish cleaned. They'll chop off the heads too, and keep them for their own devices. Have you ever seen their buckets, filled with fish-heads, eyes staring in all directions? I clean all fish the same way, slitting their bellies from neck to tail, pulling out the offal and scraping off the insides with a knife, under running water. Cleaning my own fish, gutting them, de-scaling them, keeps me in touch with the essence of the sea and all things watery. Getting my fingers messy with the yellow entrails. When I've cleaned my fish I leave the heads intact, attached to the fishes' bodies, where they belong. I sprinkle them with salt, toss some parsley over them, and put them in the cold. I find it reassuring to have something in the fridge with eyes, staring outward from the cold blind company of vegetables and dairy produce.

Swimming in a Lake

The lake is a mile long and ends in a dam. The banks are steep rubble and pine. It is overcast and thunderous. I ease myself into the water. Cold. I am out of my depth almost at once. Breaststroking out to the middle, the surface is like black ink. Or dark glass. I take long strokes, kicking wide. My nipples tingle. Head below the water with the stroke, long and slow. Breathing in, out: in, out. The ripples in the water spread gently, widening arcs in the stillness of the lake. Swimming in truly deep water starts a thrill of fear. Once I am in the centre I turn to the left and begin to swim the lake lengthways. Long, slow sweeps of the arms, head beneath the water. Up for breath, and stroke again. I open my eyes below the water and see green. I taste fresh water on my tongue. There are eyes beneath the water, other than my own. Deep and deeper goes the silence of a manmade freshwater lake in the hills. Deeper than the silence of the sea, and of rivers. Here there is a silence of imprisoned water: water collected for eventual use by city-dwellers. Water in captivity. I dare not drop deep into this water: I know those seeing, unseen things would seek me out. I keep my course, breathing steady. Long, slow strokes. Forest gliding by at water's edge. The rain takes me by surprise. Fat warm drops, a few at first. A fertile, fragrant rain. The smooth skin of the lake punctured in a million places by a rain increasing in intensity and volume, till the crescendo of the downpour is capped by a jagged stroke of lightning, and a thunder crash. I swim beneath the water.

Peeling an Orange

Peeling an orange presents a choice. Do you use a knife or fingers? Or simply cut the fruit and suck the innards from the turned-back skin, letting the bitter smoothness brush against your tongue? I often feel an urge to sink my teeth into those loose flaps of peel, and do. Fresher the orange, less need for a knife. Dig your thumb deep into the stem-joint and pull. Breaking the skin, a puff of vapour, a tiny explosion of the orange genie. Blink and you'll miss it. Don't blink and you'll sting your eyes. Pith will cling under your thumbnail, sticky and likely to irritate the tender flesh beneath the nail. The thin chunks of peel fall away like plaster. Alternatively, use a knife. In which case, most likely you will carve the skin into quarters, joining at the apex and the stem. Remember that the world is like an orange, but blue. Holding the knife steadily between middle finger and thumb, turn back the skin with the index finger, if you have one. Then what? Cut away the quarters. Eat the orange. The acidic residue sticks to the back of your teeth. The juice burns into mouth ulcers. In ancient China sorcerers would rub the peel and pith onto the glans penis of a dying man in order to achieve a favourable reincarnation. In the winter Greeks lay orange peel on top of their wood-burners. The scent welcomes the olive-pickers as they return after a day's work in the fields. Sitting down to rest their aching legs, one of them begins to peel an orange.

Baking

You pour rough-grained flour in a mixing bowl. Add a little salt. Yeast, which has been rising in a glass, warm and pungent. You mix in a scoop of margarine. Fingers like clay stalagmites whirl and pound the dough into a ball, then drop it on the table-top. Kneading begins, with knuckles, palm and fist. The mixture softens, warms beneath the pummelling, a process of invention, an unforced shaping till an elasticity develops, at which point it's time to toss it back into the mixing bowl and place it in a warm and dark environment, to let it prove. Prove what? To prove that it is probus, honest, proven, true: to prove that it is bread-to-be, a doughty dough. Proving most relates the art of making bread to alchemy, the yeast whose cells proliferate and cause the swelling, so that uncovered, the warm belly of the naked, unbaked bread sings out its own essential nature: verbitude. No verb was ever more so than dough rising. No smell was ever more associated with edible potential. Bread in the act of becoming. You knead it for a second time, rejoicing in its sensuous give. You grease a tray. Shape a loaf. Put it in the oven. Make some tea. Listen to some music. Learn from the art of becoming that is the baking of a loaf.

Restaurant

I walk past a restaurant. It is nearly midnight. A few people are eating outside. There is an atmosphere of relaxed dishevelment about the place, which I like. So I go in, take a seat. Narrow, smoke-stained ceiling. On the wall, a popular print of the parachute invasion of Crete: a blue-pantalooned partisan readies himself to slay the first descending German, helpless on the strings of his pathetic destiny.

After a while, the waiter comes to my table. He is a small man with very blue eyes and a drooping moustache. He stands in front of me, with a notepad and pencil, seemingly poised to take my order. I ask for drink and a little food. He does not acknowledge what I have said, but instead eases himself into the seat facing me, looking at me closely. He gestures to another, older man behind the counter, who brings a carafe and two glasses, a plate of food. The waiter pours drinks carefully. I notice that his hand is shaking.

Slowly, with extraordinary detail, he tells me the story of his life: how his mother died when he was three years old; the attempts of his devastated father to raise him and his sister; his ambition to be a painter; of studying in the city; his courtship and marriage; the years of hardship while his young blonde wife supported them both. How he fell from grace with god; failed as an artist; how his wife left him for a Turkish sailor; how he came to this town and found work in this restaurant.

When he finishes, the restaurant is empty. Hours have passed. The waiter gets up and goes outside to clear the tables. On leaving, the older man thanks me for listening to the waiter's story. He accepts no money.

Bees

Returning from the olive fields with nets, axe and saw, I was told that Iannis the honeymaker had been stung to death by his bees. He was a man in his early forties, with three children. He had entered the hive, in the Greek way, without protection. That evening, in the kafeneion, the shepherds sat in silence with their crooks and worry beads. In the background was a perpetual wailing that came from the direction of Iannis the honeymaker's home. Occasionally the wailing would be interrupted by screams and shouting. I imagined the beating of the widow's fists on walls, the beating of the widow's fists on unyielding hives, the beating of the widow's fists on her husband's departing back.

Then, as night fell on the mountains, a mysterious humming sound began to seep into the air. I went and stood on the veranda, overlooking the village square. People appeared in doorways, shutters were opened. The deep buzzing grew louder, a counterpoint to the shrill wailing from the dead man's house, and then, very gradually, it subsided. Nobody talked about this afterwards, but I knew from their faces the next day that everyone had heard it.

Boat Repairs

The boat was painted red and blue, and its hull needed scraping and painting with protective paint. I tied it to the winch hook and began winding it in. The wire was long and thin. The boat shuddered on the logs that we had placed under the keel, and inched forward onto dry land. A couple of the other fishermen helped me. Two carpenters from the boatbuilders' yard stood by, smoking. These two stayed away from the winch itself, pointing out, in expert voices, the scraggy condition of the taut wire, the loose bristles, the threadbare places where it seemed impossible the winch would hold. We knew that if the wire snapped back it could wrap itself around the neck and kill any one of us. The same thing happened whenever I helped to bring a boat in: speculation as to what precisely might occur to any likely victim. Accounts of what had happened at other times in other places. Reminders that as well as fishing at sea, the repair of boats was a perilous business also. But a new winch system was never introduced. That would have meant nothing to talk about when the fishermen hauled a boat in.

Paradise Bay

Looking out beyond the tiny island of Saint Nicholas, the sea a deep clear turquoise, it occurred to me that I would never want for anything, given this tiny home above the bay, a place to grow things, the scent of rosemary and the lapwing's cry. I began digging trenches early in the morning, fixed the dry-stone wall, and sorted irrigation for tomatoes. Afterwards I rolled cigarettes, drank mountain tea, wrote in my notebook with vigorous concentration. I ate outside and watched the dolphins leap below. That night I lay exhausted and at peace before a fire of olivewood. I listened to an owl and counted shooting stars, my mind ablaze with plans and poems.

But within a month bulldozers had moved in across the bay, adjacent to Manoli's restaurant. Piles of dirt and rock; cement mixers, diggers, a crew of Albanian labourers eyeing the tourist girls on day trips from the beach hotels. Foundations led to steel girders and more cement. They were building a hotel for Manoli. One afternoon I went to the restaurant, had some food, then stayed and drank till I was drunk, and then drank more.

The next day I woke in a trench of vegetable peelings outside the clifftop house, my body mottled with mysterious bruises, shirt soiled and torn. I packed and left for the city.

Bones of the Ancestors

This village by the sea: fragments of white rock in the shadow of the mountain. A deserted harbour. An old woman, dressed in black, sits knitting outside an empty house, the last remaining inhabitant. I pass inside and climb the stairs. A small room on the top floor, with a single high window. Long heaps of pebbles, at right angles to the walls. To reach the window I must climb onto one of these piles. I clamber up. A man appears in the doorway, looks sternly at me, leaves. Turning, he says a single word, containing three syllables. I look down and realise the piles are human remains, sparsely covered in rubble. This is the room of ancestors, and I am treading on their bones. Knowing I have committed an outrage, I go downstairs to where the crone sits, bearded and silent. The movement of her hands absorbs me. I feel as though this fluency, this complete and unthinking control is an allegory of her thought, and that she must be a custodian or doorkeeper. She is at once a calming and forbidding presence. I apologise for walking on the bones. I hear her say there is a man inside the house who only says one word. Any one who hears this word dies instantly. She looks up from her knitting and stares out to sea. I realise she has not looked at me, nor spoken.

Watermelons

One day in June a giant appeared on our street corner with a truckload of watermelons. With the help of the driver the fruits were unloaded onto the street in an enormous pile and the giant sat down next to them for a month, in a chair borrowed from the kafeneion across the square. At night the watermelons were covered by a grey tarpaulin. From time to time the waiter from the kafeneion would bring the giant a cup of coffee and a glass of iced water, on a tray. The giant put the tray by his feet, sipped at the coffee. He never touched the water. He was mute and unsmiling. He was never seen to eat and I never heard him speak. I bought a watermelon from him once, and he held up five fingers, indicating fifty drachmas.

One night, returning along the unlit street from the Lyrakia Bar, I pulled back the edge of the tarpaulin, intending to steal a watermelon. Peering beneath the folds of the canvas in the moonlight, I failed to identify a single fruit, but recognised instead the glint of gold, the shimmer of jewels. I stepped back in surprise, just as the giant emerged roaring in the darkness. We faced each other for a second. Then I spotted the small curved dagger in his fist, and I ran.

Late the next morning, I passed the heap of watermelons. The giant was dozing in his chair, head to one side. I noticed that he wore no jewellery. At his feet was a tray, the tiny cup with its stain of coffee grains, and the untouched glass of iced water.

Oblivion

It rained without mercy between Christmas and New Year's day. Every day the two of us played cards to see who would tramp through the wet mud to buy wine and every day I lost. On New Year's day I lost at cards again, in spite of cheating. But I refused to go and fetch the wine. I hoped a dispute might crack the tedium, but my companion, more moribund than myself, simply curled up on his bunk and went to sleep.

Outside, the farmer's bitch barked at the rain from the confines of her metal kennel. I walked out into the halflight. The blue shadow of a mountain. Rain slanting through olive groves. Beyond the trees, grey sea. Oblivion. Nothing existed outside this island. The solitary mountain, olive trees, rain, the distant sea. Somewhere, behind the rain, the bullying monologue of a chain-saw.

Shepherd

After a long day's walk I stopped at a village: the only village in that part of the mountains. It was a cold evening. The owner of the bar offered me goat meat and bread, washed down with small bottles of strong spirit. A fire burned in the brazier, which the owner fed with logs of olive wood. As night fell, the place filled with shepherds. They sat in twos and threes, smoking. Most of them ignored the blaring television, set high on the wall to the side of the bar. But there was one old shepherd with a white moustache who watched the TV, scowling angrily. The programme was presented by the talentless son of a dead and famous Hollywood star. It involved a banal parade of acts introduced by this inane male, himself surrounded by a cluster of half-dressed females who cooed and cuddled him in a state of simulated bliss. Nobody but this old man was watching the programme. I saw him trembling in rage, his hands clasping the table's edge, his eyes perplexed. He strained to read some subtitled prattling, then stood, quaking in his leather boots and overcoat. He treated the occupants of the bar to an explosion of furious dialect, and then he left. He was not embracing compromise.

On the Beach

There was a long, empty beach. No people except for me. I walked barefoot in the shallow water, up and down. A cloudy morning. Small waves broke and spilled onto the shore. Because I was not looking, I would have walked right into it. The stench made me stop in my tracks. A pair of gulls shuffled away angrily and then flew off.

At first I could not make it out. It was a great grey mess of something, encased by a dark rim. A brown carapace supported the mess, squirming with maggot life, slithering shapes burrowing and feeding in the remnants of purple and yellow flesh.

When I realised that it was a turtle, my revulsion gave way to the kind of melancholy that could only be induced by a dead and stranded creature eaten up by worms and grubs and gulls on a deserted beach.

There was nothing to do but stare at it.

Shaving a Face

The man wants to shave. He has the luxury of hot running water in his home, so he fills a basin and splashes his face. Wetting the skin eases the application of shaving cream, from a black and white plastic tube, which he squeezes carefully onto the palm of his left hand. He dabs with the fingers of the other hand and rubs the lotion onto his chin, his cheeks, the upper lip, the little hollow beneath the nose, smoothes it in luxuriously so that a thick lather covers all the area he wishes to deprive of whiskers. The growth elsewhere is not plentiful: but a three days' stubble can no longer be ignored. He uses a hand razor with a Wilkinson blade. He scrapes carefully, following the grain of the whiskers. He once overheard a conversation in a café about the need to go with the grain whilst shaving, and it stuck. He goes with the grain. The excess foam he flicks into the basin, flecked with short dark shavings. He begins below the left ear, and works from left to right, the way you read this, but he leaves the moustache till last. It is a calm process, one which he almost enjoys. He likes the feel of freshness afterwards. For several years he had a beard. Once, when he had been arrested, the bad cop had to answer the phone, and the good cop told him that what he liked most about his annual leave was this: he didn't have to shave for two whole weeks. And he didn't. It was a moment of irrelevant confession, but it lodged in the memory. Like the man in the cafe, who went with the grain.

43

Brushing Hair

I watch her brushing her daughter's hair. These fluent movements, the generous finality of each stroke, arouse in me the most precise connection with the scent of oranges and the sound of children's laughter. The mother smiles, her head tilted at a slight angle. Her legs are parted, the child leaning against a bare brown knee. She works the brush rhythmically over the long thick hair. She is singing quietly. The glide of each downward stroke is accompanied by a barely audible exhalation of the chair's woodwork. In the jungle from which the wood was cut, drums are being beaten in the hot and bloated night. Mosquitoes fill the air. The young victim, who has lived out a year as a divinity, is being prepared for sacrifice. Near to the altar, the sacred jaguar presses against the bars of her cage. At the moment the soul leaves the body, the jaguar will be set loose, tearing into the moonlit forest. She will be the carrier of divinity for a full year until a night like this, when she will be hunted down and killed. A young girl will take her place. This annual ritual celebrates the symbiosis between human culture and the forest. The girl is having her hair brushed at this moment. She is staring into the night, unafraid. She wonders what it will be like, life inside the jaguar's skin.

Moving House

They had been crossing a city wasteland. There was a lack of clean water, and absolutely no trees of any description. Vultures, perhaps. Crows, probably. Starlings, certainly, lined up in rows on the overhead wires. The locals believed them to be the souls of dead prostitutes. There was a sick and lethargic river which called to mind other sick, lethargic rivers in desolate urban settings. Once, they were told, this had been a wealthy town, to be compared with the mightiest in the empire. But the coal had stopped coming and the citizens hadn't noticed. Just as they ignored the sounds from the river when the water was high and the floods came down from the hills. Sounds that incorporated an hypnotic litany of chthonic consonants, the neighing vowels of blind ponies, and the expelled wind of drowned and inflated cattle. Once a raft-load of mountain sheep and one triumphantly barking dog came spinning down the river, on its way into the Atlantic mist. God knows. Somewhere in all this rubble there must have been a house, if not a home. They found it between a brewery, its huge chimney spewing dark vapours into the leaden afternoon sky, and a corrugated bakery, from whose ventilation system wafted the promise of unbelievably sweet cakes.

They entered the house, and recognised its breathing. It seemed as though the place had been recently abandoned. In the largest room there was a table. On it were a Spanish dictionary and a statue of the Buddha. They moved in.

Ironing

Ironing used to be a chore. Those stiff collars needing to be pressed. The shirtfronts immaculate. A thousand vests. Women facing basketloads of Monday afternoon despair. Women doing work to make their men presentable. The smell of Mondays in my own family home. Wet washing drying over radiators. Baked potatoes. Steam irons belching, hissing. Relentless cloud cover. A consistently incontinent sky. If the sun came out we'd have a public holiday. Would we hell. Rain, I'd venture, is a process. Growing up in a wet country gave me opportunity to observe this process closely. And of course, rain takes over, becomes an element of culture. Hang the washing out, bring it in when the rain comes, hang it out again, hang it in, hang it on the clothes horse that bore no resemblance to a horse. Ironing: I would admire the confident strokes, the way my mother steered around the buttons, creased the collars, turned and folded sleeves. Finished articles stacked up neatly in the airing cupboard, the warm dough of a material confection. But even ironing has changed. Now we have postmodern ironing. Men in Disney boxer shorts ironing plastic bags and posters. Naked men ironing their stomachs. Newly decapitated men ironing their hair.

Stripping Paint

Tiredness is no obstacle to imagination. And stripping this fireplace is an act of faith. The house is one hundred years old and the fireplace in the bedroom has been painted many times. Shades of yellow, grey and brown are revealed as I scrape closer to the wood. The toxic vapours of the paint-remover assault my nose and eyes. I wear a mask and goggles, and feel as though my real vocation might be to track and capture small poisonous devils, and boil them in cauldrons in the city centre. The mask is stuffy. The goggles steam up. The plastic gloves are sticky, and the mixture burns through anyway. I take off all the gear and carry on. It's good to breathe, and what are toxins anyway but necessary challenges to a healthy constitution? The bubbling paint work resembles a skin condition familiar to readers of medical encyclopaedias. I treat it with a spatula. It peels away in curling strips, dropping onto the newspaper in yellow and brown spirals. Slowly a landscape of wood appears, a rich-veined walnut, its story told by century-thick paint. Working on the ingrained stains with wire wool, my arm aching, brushing out the crevices and hollows, scraping out the concave fluting and the hidden parts below the mantelpiece. Watching the contours and whorls in the grain close-up, woodworm's eye view, the fireplace becomes the world, the world becomes the fireplace. Here fires are laid. The crackle of logs, the blue and orange flame. Smoke issues from the chimney. Along with this, a premonition of ashes and renewal.

Under the Mountain

The two men leave their car in a dark and wooded lane. They follow the track up into the mountains in the half-light of dawn. They walk purposefully, but without hurry. They are talking in clear voices, because the mountain urges them to speech, but also because the occasion demands the careful weighing of words that leave room for the sequences of ritual: the steady pace of their footfall, the reddening sky, the stirring of birds. They follow the valley, along the banks of an icy stream that narrows towards its source. Hawthorn and fern dress the valley floor. The sun crests the ridge and a sudden wind gusts at their back. They pass the ruins of a stone cottage and then the stream's banks rise sharply overhead on either side. Here there is a small waterfall, and a pool, chest-deep. The men collect firewood, and prepare rocks in a small circle. They strip off. The sun shines straight down the valley, but the breeze takes the edge off any warmth. As one man enters the pool, the other takes a hermetic jar from his knapsack. The jar is filled with fine ashes, which he pours into the palm of his free hand and onto the hands of the other man. They rub ashes vigorously into their skin: onto face, neck, chest, stomach, genitals, legs and into hair. In turn they enter the cold water. After bathing, one man sets a fire, the other stands naked, feet apart, knees and elbows bent, fists loose, rocking steadily and staring down at the mountain that rises like a woman's

breast beyond the end of the valley. He is chanting words in an imploring undertone. Behind him the fire begins to crackle and spit, flames leaping. Suddenly the standing man stops making sounds, and lowers himself to the ground, in a squatting position. His right hand settles on a clump of heather. He tears it from the ground in one swift motion. Attached to each of its meagre roots is a golden thread. The man grasps all the threads together, twisting them into a rope. He turns, standing now, and with both hands, pulls hard. The surface cracks, the dry soil scatters, and there emerges from the ground a human head, severed at the neck. The head is a mahogany colour, with fine golden hair and deep brown eyes. As the man holds it at arm's length, the head lets out a long sigh. Crumbs of soil fall from the lips.

Train

I wake up on this train. God knows where it's going. The compartment is empty. I am lying outstretched over all four seats. Dark green upholstery. My mouth is parched. I walk down the corridor. All the compartments are empty. I try the door to the next carriage. It's locked. I walk to the other end. That door too is locked. The train is racing through an unfamiliar landscape, past stations, too fast to read their names. I stand at a window, shocked by the speed. Villages, church spires. Rushing through tunnels, there is no lighting in the carriage so all is darkness, and then out again into a white sunlight. Orchards, rivers, cattle, barns. Snow-peaked mountains in the distance. What land is this? Didn't I board the train with friends? Who were they; what were their names; where are they now? What city did we leave? There is the lingering memory of a song, and this taste like sherbert in my mouth. I sit back in the compartment, put my feet on the facing seat. I give myself over to the feeling of movement. Out of half-closed eyes I notice warehouses, chimneys, pylons. They slip by like a story heard once only, in conditions not favourable to storytelling. It dawns on me, quite slowly, that this train isn't going to stop. If only I could remember. There is something that I must remember. If I do, the train will slow down, come to a stop. But I've even forgotten what it is that I'm trying to remember to remember.

Mowing the Lawn

I can see my father mowing the lawn beneath my bedroom window. It is late on a summer's afternoon. I am six years old. The hills are purple, the fields falling down to the river are lush and green. Cattle have converged near our garden fence, young bullocks. They are agitated and curious, riding each other, sliding off, rounding, charging and feinting. Cars buzz down the main road out of the village, on the straight stretch downhill, past the sawmill. What I am watching is a man and a lawnmower. Sometimes the man leads the machine, sometimes the machine leads the man. At the end of a long straight run, a sudden halt, and a turn. But the mower does not always want to turn in the same direction as the man. It jerks away, and the man wrestles with it for a second, before regaining control, and twisting it into a return. Halfway down the lawn the man is pursued by a wasp, and he strikes out at random about his face with one hand, somehow keeping the mower on course with the other. My bedroom window is open and I lean out. My elbows ache. He cannot see me, but I am watching him. Why does he walk with downcast eyes? A fly buzzes in my room, caught behind the netting. A butterfly, red and gold, jigs past. All these flying things; and how I wish the mower would take off, surge from the green domesticity of the lawn, and launch into the sky, my father attached, his legs still striding at takeoff, his arms outstretched, hanging onto the machine's hurtling green fury. I think that his face is livid with joy. They circle, reappear above the treetops, startling angry crows, and come to ground between two young cypresses.

My father pauses, wipes the sweat from his forehead with a white handkerchief embroidered with the letter 'R', though his name begins with 'C', and carries on as though nothing had happened. When I look at the lawn, I am thrilled by the symmetry of the mown grass, in alternate rows of lighter and of darker green.

Mushrooming

They held Edgar down while he was drunk, and gave him a Mohican haircut. Edgar was an aspiring clochard in his late thirties, simple minded, a holy innocent, with the mournful face of a surprised clown. He wandered the Charentes region doing agricultural work. But these young pickers, down at Cognac for the grapes, running out of things to do, had picked on him and shaved his head. And so he wore a black woolly hat, which made his clown's face all the sadder.

Edgar told us of his days doing military service. How he had to make a parachute jump, and looked out of the aeroplane in terror at the ground below. He saw, he said 'les petits bonhommes' down below. He refused to jump. The sergeant pushed him anyway. It seemed to be what people did to Edgar, always.

That Sunday I went mushrooming with Edgar, who told me that he knew a thing or two concerning funghi. He knew nothing, and we returned with a sackful of inedibles. The farmer's wife picked through our findings with nimble fingers and one after another tossed all varieties aside, as Edgar's face drooped further still in disappointment. He later confided to me that what he really knew about was fishing. His father taught him when he was a boy. Autumn in his village, people had gone hunting rabbits Sundays, or else mushrooming. But he and his father were exceptions: they were fishermen. Next Sunday, if we could only find some tackle, we would go fishing.

Saint Mont

This is the Gascon village where the alleged events took place. It was here that Isabelle's dog was run over by a Paris taxi driven by a bear. This is the bench where I settled down to sleep after a heavy meal only to be found, minutes later, drinking coffee in the Café d'Artagnan five kilometres away, a miracle observed by several witnesses. It was here, during a lunar eclipse in 1984, that a man was seen, in full crusader's outfit, nursing a mangled leg and begging for alms, while watching an Occitane game show on a portable television propped up against his shield. This is the place, in a corner of the churchyard, where the everyday becomes absorbed into a plot you can write yourself into. Just like that. It involves five maize castrators, a field, a stormy night, a Brazilian song and a small white dog. From the hilltop we can see the plains of Madiran, an area famous for its vineyards. But the production of wine is of no concern to us, except as a transforming process, a sort of alchemy. What we have come to puzzle over, sinking gently into the morning's scented calm, is why this place maintains its obvious hold on memory; why it demands a ransom from me. After all, I owe Saint Mont nothing. Do I?

Salt Thieves

Who were those men? They threw long shadows, even when the sun was high. They came into the village singly or in pairs, hung around doorways, stared awkwardly at the ground when spoken to. No one knew why they had come. It was as if they had lost something and had come back to find it, but could not find the courage to ask for help. They did not have proper language. They fumbled in their speech, producing long purring rhotics and weak babbling labials. They made only a single, pitiful vowel sound. They had an air of perpetual bewilderment. We offered them bread and bacon, but learned that they preferred it left out on the doorstep. Then they would take the food in their hands to consume greedily in some corner, like dogs. They never gained in confidence. But eventually we got used to them being around.

One night they left. No one saw them go, but in the morning there was no trace of them. And every household was suddenly bereft of salt. No signs of theft or break-in. We thought it strange that they should want our salt: strange too, the following year, when ungainly desert plants began to grow at isolated spots around the place, on street corners and in doorways. Singly or in pairs.

Deep Song

In the amber city, wandering through streets too narrow for
sunlight, the chime of church bells conveying a dense
frustration, I came across a beggar without a nose, who
begged a coin. I stopped to speak with him, a youngish
man, with long, dirty hair. He smelled of rotting flesh. I
asked what he would do with the money if I gave him
some. He said he would buy wine and cigarettes. I said, in
that case go, but buy two bottles, one for you, and one for
me, and come back to this shady spot so we can drink
together. He shuffled off, dragging one foot.

When the beggar returned, minutes later, his demeanour
had changed entirely. He approached waving the bottles at
me, grinning wildly. He was very low on teeth. He sat
beside me in the doorway of a disused church, and as he
stooped I noticed that his nearside ear was missing. Lighting
a cigarette I could not fail to observe that he only had three
fingers on the left hand, two on the right. It occurred to me
that this was a person in the very process of disintegration.

The beggar and I drank, talking little, but I gathered he was
from the South. After a while we needed to refill our bottles
and walked together to the little store. On our return the
tramp began to sing, deep song, a rich exuberance of sound,
there in the shady alley with the watching cats and this
sense of always returning to the same place: the pissed-on
mattress piled against the wall, the litter of empty cartons.
And this singer prince who had been assigned the

kingdom of the gutter.

I walked away, the singer in mid-song, eyes closed. He would never notice I was gone. It was not his job to notice other people's comings and goings.

High Plateau

There is no landscape so bereft of verbs as this high plateau. Wind; a wind that sculpts the peaks and gullies into a frozen seascape. I can't remember how I got here. I guess I must have walked. A hundred metres from the roadside, near a shell-struck shack, I awaken with the pale sun in my eyes. It is cold. It could be morning or evening. I have no sense of direction. An untethered goat stares at me, then bleats and runs away. I stand stiffly. My feet are blistered. A few battered trees, scrubland. Did I dream that a stranger approached me as I slept, asked me questions? The debris of a week's hallucinations, fragments from a journey with no map. Where did I set out? Who brought me to this place? These questions take on significance for a few brief moments, and then become irrelevant. I cannot concentrate for long enough to absorb the impact of a single thought. I need a drink. I piss, in a hot steaming arc, the only movement here, my neck and shoulders knotted. Then I hear the sound of a car in the distance, climbing the long hill to this high plateau. I walk towards the road.

Tourism

Tourism is a metaphor for apocalypse. On the second day of August, the rainclouds opened and the city soaked. The narrow twisting lanes in the old quarter turned into cataracts within minutes. Outside the inexplicably closed cathedral, parties of Germans, British, Americans and Japanese clutched hats and maps against the downpour. Just along, where the lanes begin, crouched a beggar, draped in a shapeless grey garment, oblivious to inclemencies of weather. She has been sitting here for centuries. A raven hops nervously on her shoulder. It croaks in her ear from time to time, and the beggar, irritated by the bird's noisy presence, attempts to brush it away with angry shooing gestures. The bird, however, is persistent: this is its function. It knows its pivotal role in this drama. Without the bird there would be no beggar. Without the beggar there would be no cathedral. Without the cathedral there would be no tourists.

Synchronicity

Here's what happened. Antonio Machado, celebrated Spanish poet, was fleeing Spain and the advancing Francoist army. After a desperate journey through a defeated Catalunya, he arrived at the French border village of Cerbère. It was raining heavily. The authorities would not let him into France. His papers, they said, were not in order. Soaking wet and sick, Machado took refuge in a small hotel in nearby Collioure. He left the building once only, to watch the fishing boats in the small harbour. Shortly afterwards, he died. It was Ash Wednesday, 1939.

The following year, Walter Benjamin, the noted German polymath and essayist, arrived in Cerbère, coming from the opposite direction. He was fleeing the Nazis, trying to get to Spain. From Spain he hoped to catch a boat to America. The authorities would not let him leave France. His papers, they said, were not in order. Despairing at the state of the Europe he could not leave, while eluding the holocaust of which he would no doubt have been a victim, Benjamin chose to take his own life, using poison.

Antonio Machado was born on the same day – July 26th 1875 – as Carl Jung, the originator of the theory of synchronicity. Walter Benjamin had a low opinion of Jung, considering him to be a supporter of the Aryan myth, and accusing him of doing 'the devil's work'.

Dogshit Alley

It was my first and only visit to the artist's apartment. He lived on the top floor. His studio offered a sensational view of the Alhambra. But first, he said, we had to negotiate dogshit alley. The artist spoke of it like one describing a secret shame. There was nothing he could do. On the third floor lived a resident who kept a wolfhound. She never exercised the dog, and let him use the landing as a toilet, which he did, prolifically. Formerly, the top flat had been empty, and no one came to visit the woman and her gawking beast. Now the artist was installed above her, and the woman had adopted the stance of long-term resident with rights. The dog, she said, harmed nobody. She seemed oblivious to the smell. The artist could not confront her. Each time he passed the landing he felt like vomiting. He tried speaking with the woman. She would stand in the doorway, the hound slavering and growling at her side. 'Look' she said, smiling meekly: 'he wouldn't hurt a fly. He's an old softie'. She ruffled the grey fur on his head, and an incredibly long tongue flicked out and caressed the underside of her wrist. The woman smelled of gin, had white hair, parchment skin, and the smile of a ten year old. 'He hates going out, see. He gets so scared'. The artist was lost for words. He told me: 'I don't know what to say to her'.

When we climbed the stairs to the third floor, the stench suddenly hit me. I held a handkerchief to my nose. We navigated the landing, stepping over mountainous turds. I didn't breathe until we reached the attic studio, and walked out into the clean December air. The Alhambra stood magnificent against the backdrop of the Sierra: an impeccable statement that made me realise that it is the reproduction of a clichéd image that renders a cliché, and not the original. 'You see', said the artist, 'I just don't know how to deal with her at all'. He lived in the house of a thousand turds with a dying woman and an agoraphobic wolfhound for neighbours. This was the artist's quandary and he could not resolve it.

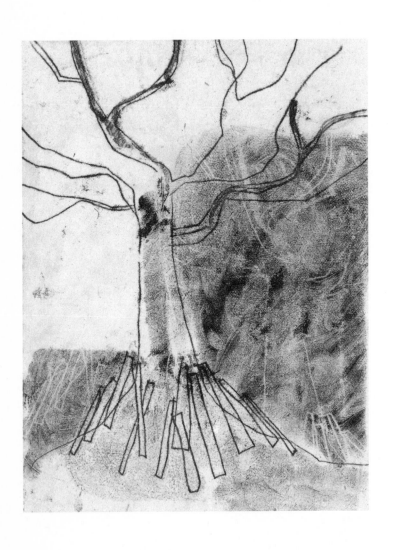

Chopping Wood

An old man descends the wide cobbled steps: in his hand a large white sack. He sits beneath the plane tree and takes from the sack two objects; a cushion and an axe. He then upturns the sack and blocks of wood in various shapes tumble onto the ground. The blocks are square, rectangular, irregular, dense. He sits carefully on the cushion and begins to split the blocks into fine short staves. These he piles neatly at the base of the tree. He neither smokes nor hums as he works: nor does he whistle, nor make nervous gestures. He cuts the wood impeccably, never needing two strokes to make a clean break. His hand does not tremble. An old woman, black-clad, approaches, bird-like. She carries a bulging black bag. The man stands and empties the contents onto the cobbles. More blocks of wood. Without a word he leaves his own stack and begins to chop the new assignment. Mechanically, the splinters fall away, of equal size, with each vertical movement of the arm. When he has finished he puts the woman's firewood back into the black bag and hands it to her. She thanks him, with a nod of the head. He says nothing. He returns to his own, unfinished pile, and with the same unhurried motions completes his task. It has begun to rain lightly, and with the first drops the scent of hyacinths begins to drift across the little square. The man arranges the stack of kindling as close as he can to the foot of the tree so that the trunk is entirely encircled by sticks. Standing, he returns the cushion and the axe into the white sack, which he shoulders. He leaves.

Vegetable Poet   *for David Greenslade*

Pulling away the cloth which serves as a dust cover, you display an entirely promiscuous array of vegetables, and then introduce each one as though it were a subterfuge or trope. Leeks, yams, onions, peas, radish, okra, parsnip take on significances I barely guessed at that night when you invited me into your kitchen and showed me four or five magnificent carrots, thickly encrusted with rich alluvial soil, lying on top of an already crowded vegetable basket. It was an autumn night of wind and driving rain. Your children were asleep upstairs. The kitchen was dimly lit, and in the hearth a coal fire burned. I remember both my astonishment, and the flutter of an almost imperceptible loss as you carefully placed the largest carrot in the centre of the fire. Partly I was shocked at the potlatch profligacy of this pyromanic act; but more, I was filled with an imploding tearfulness, a wintry reminder of the need for sacrifice as the painful precursor to any vegetable prosperity. Just as the dying carrot glowed in the hearth, a charred phallus in the wide silence of your kitchen, I heard its weird humming, its batlike scream.

Mopping

In the hierarchy of household cleaning implements, the old-fashioned mop is queen. A hundred threads of twisted, matted cotton: a kitchen Medusa. The water must be hot, close to boiling, especially in a cold climate. The movements must be calm, slow and rhythmic, but executed with enough force to remove the more impervious marks. Mopping with amphetamine ferocity, arms pumping, head down, this is the route to an early grave, the way mopping is done in jails and addiction treatment centres. Preserve me from the Woolworths mop, with its tatty strips of blue and white cloth, its red plastic handle, the knowledge that if you squeeze it out with any passion it will snap in your arms. A broken plastic mop clutters the soul in the same way as abandoned deck-chairs on a winter beach.

It is easy, but perilous, to be led by the mop, resulting in a lazy action and a dirty floor. This is the will of the mop at work. The mop can seduce with its sensuous reach, its cheeky mop-head (once used in derogatory reference to beatniks but now sounding more like an endearment), its warm and often fragrant wetness. But a cold, damp, dirty mop is like the rejected victim of sexual abuse in a family of fundamentalists. Like most nouns, the mop is only really itself in its verbal form. Doing justifies its being.

Waking

Border country. Evening. I sit in the woods above my sister's house. The border passes through her land, an invisible boundary. How to define its nature? A border is an idea wedded to a geography. It implies a shift of consciousness, a change of order. That is why the light is as it is; shadowy, circumspect, dappled now that there is weather. It skirts a quiet and ceremonious landscape in which to bury things; treasured artefacts, memory, the particles left behind on waking. Dream sediment. This is a zone of curtains and unseen partitions. A landscape which provides the thread between the deep uncertainty of sleep and the fragile certainty of waking. Wandering along this borderline, following the trail between one country and another, is all I've ever done.

Cormorant

My father told me that a cormorant had been sighted on Crickhowell bridge, some thirty miles upriver from the Usk's confluence with the Severn. The news affected me with a jolt, took me unawares, and I almost said, without knowing why: 'Well that's it then, it's all over'. That dark brooding creature breaking new paths within these waterways signalled a subtle finality: a bird blinking on the bulwarks of a bridge that none of its breed had stood on in five hundred years, its head erect, shuffling to redistribute its bulk on the narrow wall; waiting, waiting.

Tessa Waite was born in Edinburgh in 1960 and grew up in Norwich. She gained a degree at Canterbury College of Art and an M.A. in Fine Art at Cardiff. For four years she was artist in residence at Mid Wales Psychiatric Hospital, which re-confirmed her belief in the creative potential of people even in extreme adversity. There followed a period as visiting artist in Rajasthan, Northwest India, which made a lasting impression on her. Her paintings have a lyricism which, combined with her subtle use of materials and poetic imagery, give her work a unique dynamism. She has exhibited widely with works in several major collections. Tessa Waite lives in Brecon with her husband and two children.